MCMLII
E II R
MMXII

RS

CONDITOR·HORTI·FELICITATIS·AVCTOR

The Lady Torrod-Shell

PAX·INTRANTIBVS

Remaking a Garden

The Laskett Transformed

Remaking
a Garden

The Laskett
Transformed

ROY STRONG

PHOTOGRAPHS BY
CLIVE BOURSNELL

F

FRANCES LINCOLN LIMITED
PUBLISHERS

Frances Lincoln Limited
74–77 White Lion Street, London N1 9PF
www.franceslincoln.com

Remaking a Garden
Copyright © Frances Lincoln Limited 2014
Text © Roy Strong 2014
Photographs © Clive Boursnell 2014

First Frances Lincoln edition 2014

A catalogue record for this book is available
from the British Library.

978-0-7112-3396-6

2 3 4 5 6 7 8 9

FOR SHAUN CADMAN AND PHILIP TEAGUE
without whom there would be no Laskett gardens

... a circlin[g]
Of goodliest Trees loade[d]
Blossoms and Fruits a[t]
[...]peard with ga[...]

CONTENTS

PHOTOGRAPHER'S FOREWORD

I first photographed The Laskett in the mid-1990s. I remember being totally enthralled by the garden and the personal story it told.

In 2004 I was lucky enough to be asked to photograph the garden throughout the year, to illustrate twelve monthly articles written by Sir Roy for *Country Life* magazine. In the course of that year I came to know and love the garden. Something else also became evident during that time: here was a man in his late sixties, not long widowed, with a four-acre garden he had created together with his late wife, having to come to terms with the fact that the garden had become much overgrown and was rapidly closing in on itself.

What was to be done? I suspect that most people in Sir Roy's position, with a garden carrying that kind of history, might have turned away or just left it as it was. Not Sir Roy. I much admire him for his courage in moving the garden on, and I wanted to be part of those changes. So I suggested to him that we might do a book together. This would give me the opportunity to photograph the garden in all its moods and seasons and in different lights; most importantly, I wanted to photograph the work of changing the garden.

I have been photographing gardens for a very long time. Sometimes I have only had a couple of hours to do the job, just time for a snapshot. It was a wonderful privilege to be able to photograph the life and work of a changing garden over several

years. And here I have been most fortunate in gaining the trust first of the gardeners and then of the rest of the workforce. It was a joy to wake up in my camper bus an hour before dawn, winter and summer, aware that though I knew the garden so well, each day's photography would bring something new I had not seen before. Unencumbered by my past work in the garden I treated each day's photography totally on its own merits, treasuring the freedom to capture the best pictures for that day. I tried always to see as if for the very first time the light and the mood of the garden, the planting that was to the fore, the process and progress of work by the gardeners, builders, tree surgeons. I never once pre-edited my shoot and never said to myself, 'I've done this before' (although of course I carried with me a knowledge of past shoots). The photography was always full on, without interference. It was a massive subject and I was always refining what I'd done and seeking the one picture that would hold the essence of the whole work.

I could never have worked on this project, no matter the depth of my passion, without the generous consent of Sir Roy, and without the trust given to me by the head gardener, Shaun Cadman, and by his right-hand man, Philip Teague. Thanks also to Geoff and Gerry Davies, the first builders, and to their successors Tom and K. Macklin and Alvin Blewitt and his brother; to painters Paul Reeks and his son Chris; to tree surgeons Chris and Nick Mawdsley, Charles Smith, Dave Fissenden and Rob Smith; to Alan and Tom Loveridge, who made the new paths and laid the drainage; to Reg Boulton, creator of plaques and stone lettering, and his successor Catriona Cartwright; to Fiona Fyshe, for her ever-flexible Café Laskett; to portrait painter Paul Brason, for the helicopter ride over The Laskett; to part-time gardener Shane Teague; to Simon Abbis and his wife, apple-picker and juicer, who appeared on my very last day of shooting, 1 October 2013; and to dear Maisie, dog, and dearest Katie, cat.

Away from the garden, to Tom Miller, for photo-technical support; to Nicola Davies, Jilly Forster, and Jack and Joyce Edelman for asking why; to Jo Christian, our editor, so patient with me; to Becky Clarke, my art director, for her brilliant design work; and above all, always, to Barbara.

Thank you all.

Clive Boursnell
London, October 2013

It was the photographer Clive Boursnell's inspired idea that he should record the action of what might be described as the remaking of a garden. Admittedly, many gardens have been recorded several times over the years, but that has been in the main in a haphazard way. As far as I know, no one has recorded this process so methodically. 'Action' is the significant word here. Clive has captured not only the scene as it was and as it has become but also its gradual transformation at the hands of the gardeners, builders, tree surgeons and painters who worked on The Laskett gardens over a decade. In that sense the book is his, and a first.

But what has been applied in this particular garden has a message for anyone who has a garden, and of whatever size. That is that gardening is about change; and, from time to time, about quite radical change. The message to those who question whether to make such changes is not to hesitate but be bold. Gardening is like a picture that is never finished, one that is forever calling for alteration and retouching. Growth and the seasons, not to mention the vagaries of fashion, render it a mutant art.

It is also one which is a collective endeavour, for the eye of the maker calls for those on the workshop floor to share in the vision and turn it into reality. That is why the images of those I've called here 'The Cast' are an essential part of the story.

But for that story to become a book there has to be as its bedrock the work of a photographer prepared to enter into an extraordinary level of commitment over a long a period of time. It is Clive's pictures that tell the story.

Roy Strong
The Laskett, October 2013

The gang: Shaun, Fiona, Roy and Philip.

PLAN OF
THE GARDENS

The House

Colonnade Court

The V & A Temple

Memorial Urn

Muff Monument

Shakespeare Monument

Jonathan Myles-Lea's plan of the gardens, first drawn in 2010, here as updated in 2013.

The Stag

Hilliard Garden

Yew Garden

Key

1. Yew Garden
2. Torte's Garden
3. Glyndebourne
4. Spring Garden
5. Howdah Garden
6. Fountain Court
7. Silver Jubilee Garden
8. Pierpont Morgan Rose Garden
9. Scandinavian Grove
10. Parnassus
11. Elizabeth Tudor Walk
12. Herb Garden
13. The New Border
14. The Serpentine
15. Hilliard Garden
16. Birthday Garden
17. Beaton Bridge
18. Ashton Arbour
19. Covent Garden
20. Christmas Orchard
21. Colonnade Court

a. Lion
b. Pinnacle
c. Flora
d. Pillars of Hercules
e. Inset Roundel
f. Sundial
g. Triumphal Arch
h. Muff's Monument
i. The Crowned Column
j. Shakespeare Monument
k. Diamond Jubilee Urn
l. Gardener
m. Rose & Crown
n. Britannia
o. Unknown King
p. V & A Museum Temple
q. Henry III
r. Arms of Edward I
s. Reclining Stag
t. Headstone for Larkin & Souci
u. Memorial Urn

Triumphal Arch

Beaton Sundial

The map labels: TATIANA'S WALK · WC · The Canal · The HOUSE · Die Fledermaus Walk · SIR MUFF'S PARADE · THE DRIVE · GLADE GARDEN · SHOP · LASKETT LANE · LOWER WALK · AVENUE

The
LASKETT GARDENS
Herefordshire

HOMO SVM

R

Drawn by
Jonathan Myles-Lea

Fountain Court

Elizabeth Tudor Avenue with Crowned Column

Pierpont Morgan Rose Garden

THE LASKETT GARDENS

What does it mean to remake a garden? And why is remaking needed? I have grown increasingly aware of how people become 'blind' to their own gardens, unable to stand back and reassess their creation, often paralyzed at the very idea of altering it, indeed of removing even a single item which they have planted. This book tells the story of a particular garden but its message is one for all garden-makers. Do not be afraid to change your garden – indeed to be quite brutal to it – in order to give it new energy and excitement. After several years even a garden which you have created from scratch needs radical rethinking. Trees and shrubs have grown too large, hedges have edged their way up, vistas have vanished – the list is endless. If you have taken photographs over the years, you will be astonished to see how it has altered. In these pages you will discover how one person went about that process of restoring order and revivifying a thirty-year-old garden. Unusually – perhaps uniquely – the reader can trace the implementation of the change not only in a series of before-and-after photographs but, more importantly, in action shots.

In order to understand the need to edit a garden it is essential to know something of its history. We need to begin at the beginning. When we arrived at The Laskett in May 1973 there was no intention of making an important garden. Indeed I recall saying to my wife, shortly after we acquired the house, 'Don't talk to me about that garden.' That garden then consisted of an area around the house with lawns, a shrubbery and a rose bed. On the west side there was a small kitchen garden. The garden's most distinctive and venerable feature was a huge cedar of Lebanon planted – we were later to learn from a tree expert – about 1870. Apart from that, in terms of trees the beginning was unpropitious, for this was the era of the dreaded elm disease and our first melancholy task was to take down nine of them. Not long after that we had to remove the chestnuts up the drive, which were dead or dying, and then, in the drought of 1976, we lost a wonderful beech tree close to the house.

But where, you may ask, is The Laskett? It is situated in the village of Much Birch, midway between Ross-on-Wye and Hereford, in the county of Herefordshire. This is a beautiful county which endears itself more to me as I get older. The landscape is rolling, rugged and verdant. It is as famous for its cattle as for its cider apples. The domain which we had acquired was a triangle of land which bordered on three parishes; hence the name, which means 'a strip of land without the parish'. Most of our almost four acres stretched to the left of the drive and took the form of a field let to a farmer for his cattle. This was and still is referred to as the Field. Although we made rudimentary tinkerings with the garden in 1973, our focus was inevitably on the house and what was needed to make it fit our existence. That was to change dramatically in the summer of the following year, when the farmer announced that he no longer wished to rent the Field. By then the opportunities this might offer in terms of creating a country house garden had already crossed my mind. This was the year in which I became Director of the Victoria & Albert Museum and the one when I staged the landmark exhibition *The Destruction of the Country*

Aerial view of the gardens, 2005.

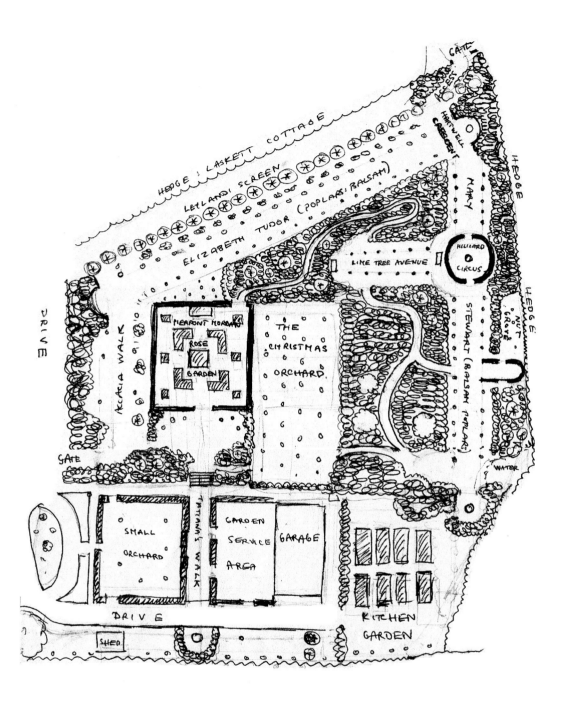

House. This lament for the loss of some thousand houses and the threat to those that remained made a forceful impression on me and, I came to realize, on others.

No garden is conceived without a complex of motives driving the makers. In my case the immemorial tradition of the country house garden, symbol of the English Arcadian vision, was certainly one. As the clouds of inflation and industrial and social turbulence gathered, I recalled the Cavaliers who, defeated in the Civil War, retreated to their estates and made gardens, in the hope that better times would return. John Evelyn and Sir Thomas Hanmer, both great horticulturists of the era, were very much in my mind. In that way from its inception what became the Laskett gardens was a pledge to the future – although in 1974, which was when we

started in earnest, no one could foresee where that path would eventually lead.

Looking back I realize that we should have asked for planning permission, but the idea that such a thing was required never crossed our minds. Julia cleverly spotted that there had once been a grass tennis court in the Field. So we had the grass mown back and it was there in December 1974 that the first of our many yew hedges was planted, to define what was to become the Pierpont Morgan Rose Garden.

As a couple we were not ill equipped to make a garden. My wife, the distinguished theatre designer Julia Trevelyan Oman, brought to it her plant knowledge from her parents' garden at Putney as well as her design skills. She was then at the height of her career, working on a series of legendary productions at the Royal Opera House, Covent Garden. I had in fact married the profession I most wanted to pursue (I ended up directing museums instead). The garden at The Laskett was in a sense to become a compensation for that loss, for it suddenly gave me full rein for a theatricality of vision which was to be fuelled by the discovery of garden history.

At this point, as I began to explore the principles of garden design, I realized that we had bought the wrong house. Ideally the house should have been at the centre of the composition, surrounded by formal enclosures and vistas dissolving into shrubbery and woodland. However, in the long term this inability to reduce the terrain in the accepted manner worked to our advantage: the Field could contain our wildest fantasies – which were far too grand for what was essentially an early Victorian sandstone box.

By then I at least had a definite idea as to the kind of garden I wanted. Julia equally, with her keen sense of practicalities, began mapping out a kitchen garden and an orchard. The Laskett gardens began to emerge, from a confluence of influences.

Hidcote, that glorious garden laid out in the Cotswolds by Lawrence Johnston before 1914, was certainly one of the prime sources of inspiration. We were lucky enough to be taken there on a frosty January day. If a garden looks good in winter it will be pleasing at any time of the year. Flowers suddenly seemed so much embroidery. What Hidcote showed me was that I had to make a plan. It taught me about ascents and descents, about contrasting enclosures and the importance of surprise. It was through Hidcote that I was drawn back to the gardens of the Arts and Crafts movement, as enshrined in one book in particular, *Gardens for Small Country Houses* by Gertrude Jekyll and Lawrence Weaver (1912).

As an Elizabethan scholar I was automatically attracted to formality, to the architectural garden and along with it topiary, knot gardens, avenues and parterres, all very out of fashion in the post-war period. Engravings by Kip in his *Britannia Illustrata* (1708), depicting the gardens of the great houses of late Stuart England, haunted me with their magnificent manipulation of vista. How could they be equalled? A visit to Cranborne Manor, the creation of the present Dowager Marchioness of Salisbury, showed me that Tudor and Stuart style could be miniaturized. Lady Salisbury offered encouragement, as also did John and Myfanwy Piper, whose kitchen garden at Fawley Bottom just outside Henley, an orderly and entrancing muddle of produce and flowers, provided a template for the importance of the garden to the kitchen.

Inevitably we began by laying out the garden around the house. The only space I could align with the house was on the east side, the site of the original Victorian garden but, by the time we arrived, reduced to a sheet of grass. During December 1974 we planted yew hedges to enclose it. This was to be the Yew Garden. Gradually and tentatively I began to colonize the grass at the centre and it was there that I planted my first dwarf box, in the form of our initials. That was to expand until, by the 1990s, this part of the garden had become one large box parterre – only to be destroyed

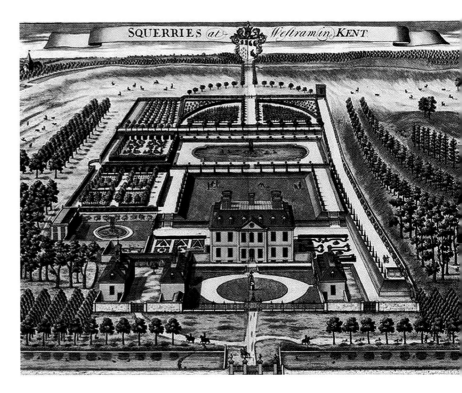

An engraving by Kip in his *Britannia Illustrata* (1708).

by the one of the earliest manifestations of the now ubiquitous box disease, *Cylindrocladium buxicola*. It was in the Yew Garden too that my earliest experiments with placing reproduction garden ornaments took place, as urns and obelisks were moved around – the gardeners saying, 'We won't cement it down Dr Strong. We know you, you'll move it.' How right they were.

My earliest plans of the Field are dated 1975 and, although the garden now is far more complex, its structural allocation of space has never fundamentally changed. There was always to be a grand avenue along what was the southern boundary. Beyond that we planted a huge leylandii hedge to shut out the Folly, the cottage which we were not to own until the 1990s. Being ignorant, we took the advice of a nurseryman anxious for a sale and initially planted an avenue of poplars. I soon realized what a disaster they were and they were quickly moved to the garden's western boundary, to act as a barrier against the winds that came across the Black Mountains. We were then advised to plant New Zealand beeches. They all perished in the great frost of the winter of 1981–82. By this time my sights had gone up in the garden world and I planted the present pleached limes, *Tilia platyphyllos* 'Rubra'. I was inspired by Sissinghurst's Lime Walk, but our avenue was to be twice the length. The second avenue ran north–south and was interrupted halfway along by a circle of yew defining what was later to become the Hilliard Garden. All of these grandiose vistas worked from the premise that sooner or later some magnificent and large ornaments would come our way to terminate them. And so in due course they did: the Shakespeare Monument, which we placed

The Yew Garden, 1975.

Making the Serpentine Walk, 1975.

at the intersection of the two avenues in 1980, and the Victoria & Albert Museum Temple, placed in 1989 to mark the northern end of the north–south avenue. What I did not know was that the chance planting of these two great arteries not at right angles was to add greatly to their attraction.

The Rose Garden, the starting point of the ground plan for the Field, was complemented by the Christmas Orchard, also planted in December 1974. Four years later I was to add an irregular yew hedge to enclose it and, at the same time, define its entrances and exits and axes. In this part of the garden there were two axes. The first, running north–south, we marked at the northern end by a statue of a recumbent stag with gilded antlers (at the southern end, but much later, we placed a statue of Britannia). The second ran west–east from the Ashton Arbour, planted in 1976 when Julia was working on Sir Frederick Ashton's ballet *A Month in the Country*. Fred would regularly ask how his arbour was coming along, and later two plaques were added to record its link with Julia's work for him, with inscriptions recording not only *Month* but also *Enigma Variations*, which had been Julia's idea for a ballet. That axis ran through a topiary tableau, inevitably called Covent Garden, and eventually (but not until the 1990s) was extended to furnish a glimpse of the Rose Garden.

Three years on from some of these initial plantings the space before the Rose Garden was laid out as a garden in celebration of the Queen's Silver Jubilee. I recall telling her at some ghastly reception for civil servants at the Palace that I had planted this garden. At that time I was in the grip of Sissinghurst, so it began its life as a white garden – a short-lived one, as I rapidly realized how uninteresting this colour scheme was and moved on to introducing

shades of violet and purple. Its present focal point came in 1981 when I purchased a sundial from the sale of Cecil Beaton's effects at Reddish House, Broad Chalke. That had been at the centre of the little lavender garden he had made during the period when I used to stay with him. At the same time I added to the garden one of his favourite roses, the repeat-flowering 'Iceberg'.

As all these enclosures took shape there remained a large irregular space. My treatment of that was inspired by plans I had studied of what was known in Stuart formal gardens as a wilderness, an enclosure with winding walks that sharply contrasted with the straight *allées* which then articulated the majority of any garden. What this signalled was a determination that the Laskett gardens were not wholly to be ruled by straight lines. In 1975 we laid out the winding Serpentine Walk. This was initially flanked on either side by flower borders, but they were quickly abandoned as impossible at that stage to maintain and the walk became instead a meandering grass path, edged with spring flowers and backed by a dense shrubbery. At that period, when everything was only a few feet high, there was an excitement in the anticipation of blocking views in the interests of surprise.

At this point a question might be asked: what resources did we have at our disposal for what was rapidly becoming a grandiose scheme? In 1974, when we began, my annual salary as Director of the Victoria & Albert Museum was £9,000, with no allowances. The pay of theatre designers was derisory, and they earned no royalties on any production. For one of Julia's major productions at the Royal Opera House, including those still in their repertory decades later, she would be paid about £12,000. So this was gardening on a shoestring. What was in our favour was the fact

The vista along Tatiana's Walk to the Silver Jubilee Garden, 1977.

Making the Silver Jubilee Garden, 1977.

that plants were cheap in the 1970s. But I cannot conceal the fact that it was a struggle to keep going.

Still, I never cut the grass. In this phase we had two gardeners, David and Wilf. They came for one day a fortnight and, if I was lucky, one of them would come for another day in between. In the winter months they went on to what were called projects and it was thanks to them that, in 1985, the Hilliard Garden was paved, together with the Birthday Garden below it, and, in 1988, the Victoria & Albert Museum Temple arose as the culmination of the great north–south vista. By then other serious pieces of garden sculpture had come our way from Julia's family. First the urn which graces the Rose Garden came to us on the death of her aunt, the author Carola Oman, Lady Lenanton, in 1978. Then when her father died in 1982 we inherited the pinnacle from All Souls and the lion from the Houses of Parliament, both of which had been at Frewin Hall, the Oxford house of Sir Charles Oman, Julia's grandfather. Knowing that these would eventually come to The Laskett, I had provided settings with their arrival in mind.

From as early as 1975 The Laskett gardens showed signs of a certain quirkiness, of a kind which was only really to hit home as being unusual after we had opened to the public. On the earliest plan of the garden in 1975, the initial two great avenues had been labelled Elizabeth Tudor and Mary Stewart, inspired by the fact that in that and the previous year we had combined to produce two little books, one on each of the two queens. Elizabeth Tudor has stuck, a single visual statement, but Mary Stewart developed over the decades into an unfolding sequence of visual experiences, each with its own identity. In this book, for clarity, I have rechristened it the Great Ascent. From there on this approach rapidly developed

into something resembling a mnemonic system – one which might seem eccentric to others but came very naturally to two people whose whole lives were entwined with the arts. When the garden opened to the public, people were naturally bewildered by, for instance, two walks named Die Fledermaus and Tatiana (from *Eugene Onegin*); but they marked two of Julia's productions at the Royal Opera House. Often, too, names arrived because a book of mine paid for this or that part of the garden. The Hilliard Garden was made possible through a little book on the Elizabethan miniaturist which appeared in 1976, the Pierpont Morgan Rose Garden marked the Walls lectures I delivered at the Pierpont Morgan Library in 1974, the Beaton Bridge marked *Cecil Beaton: The Royal Portraits* in 1989. Julia was very proud of her family – both sides, Omans and Trevelyans – so there are fair numbers of them scattered around, enshrined in such names as the Winter Rose Walk, named after Emily Winter Rose, half-sister of Julia's great-grandmother and wife of James Anderson Rose, the great patron of Rossetti.

As I am a monarchist at heart, there are celebrations also of the Queen's reign, with the Silver Jubilee Garden in 1977, the Crowned Pillar for the Golden Jubilee in 2002 and, taking the story forwards, the Diamond Jubilee Urn for 2012. Such celebrations also place the garden in time as being Elizabethan, a creation of the reign of Elizabeth II but one which looks back to that of Elizabeth I, about whom I have written so much.

I had always left blank the junction of Elizabeth Tudor and the Great Ascent, knowing that it called for something large which would one day come. And indeed it did, when in 1980 I was awarded the Shakespeare Prize by the FVS Foundation of

Hamburg. That was given each year for over half a century to the one British person considered to have done the most for the arts and I am, as far as I know, the only museum person ever to have received it. The list of recipients is an amazing one, including Henry Moore, Margot Fonteyn, Doris Lessing, Harold Pinter, David Hockney. I felt very honoured to become part of such a gathering. At the great lunch given when the prize was presented, I got up and said that this would be celebrated in the garden, and so it is. The Shakespeare Monument, a reproduction of an urn by William Kent at Longleat, was customized by way of added plaques by Reg Boulton and also by painting it in shades of terracotta and stone.

That 'fudging' up of garden ornaments is typical of this garden, the unashamed use by two people with little money at their disposal of reproduction obelisks, urns, finials and anything else which, with a bit of ingenuity, could take on another identity. In that sense it heightens the theatricality of the garden, reminding one of the work of designers like Oliver Messel who were adept at creating optical illusions from nothing much. To them I would add that inventor of architectural salvage Clough Williams-Ellis, whose Portmeirion is a monument to bric-a-brac illusion. Both are certainly clues as to how to look at the gardens of The Laskett, for in them I have been able to live out my fantasy career as a designer in the theatre. The gardens also fit in neatly with the exhibitions I staged, above all *The Elizabethan Image* at Tate Britain (1969), and the academic labour expended on the vast catalogue of the masque designs of Inigo Jones for the Stuart court.

From the outset we thought of the garden as being somehow autobiographical, in a haphazard way, about both of us. Hence, in 1988, the Greek inscription on the Victoria & Albert Museum Temple, 'Memory Mother of the Muses'. The Muses live in a museum and these gardens are all about memory – not only in the form of tangible ornaments and locations but also through plants. As I walk through the gardens friends spring to mind. The brilliant scarlet poppies came from Julia's parents' house at Putney and they remind me of their kindliness to me, the man who ran off with their daughter. Two plants above all others were sacred to Julia. The first was the quince tree whose ancestor grew at her grandfather's house, Frewin Hall, in the late Victorian period. Slips of that tree came on the removal van that brought our furniture here in 1973. Rosemary had a special meaning, for the original plant came from my mother-in-law's nanny, called Dooks, who in a very real sense 'mothered' the eight Trevelyan children after their mother died (to be succeeded by a far from loving stepmother).

Rosemary Verey is all over the garden. That friendship went back to the landmark *The Garden* exhibition at the V&A in 1979. We never came back from her celebrated garden at Barnsley without our car boot filled with plants and our minds buzzing with new ideas for our garden. It was through her that box became a favourite, and her knot inspired the one here. And once she gave me some splendid golden hollies which over nearly thirty years I

have trained into stunning topiary pieces. She would have passions for this or that plant, the last I remember being golden privet, very out of fashion at the time. Rosemary was the great encourager, and when I was asked whether I would write a book on small garden design she dispelled any hesitation that I had. She was the first person to write The Laskett gardens up in 1987 and their first appearance in any book was in her *The Garden in Winter* (1987).

But, of course, there are others. 'Iceberg' roses, as already mentioned, always recall Cecil Beaton, who helped set me on my career in the late 1960s. To our neighbour George Clive, whose estate boasted the most wonderful collection of magnolias, we owe the cowslips which have spread through the garden. One day he arrived with a great lump of Whitfield turf and from that they spawned. The huge perennial *Inula magnifica*, with its large leaves and starry bright yellow flowers, recalls a memorable visit to the great gardener and garden writer Christopher Lloyd (always referred to by Penelope Hobhouse as 'God'). The list could be multiplied, but these few reflect what so many gardeners cherish, what my mother-in-law called her 'garden of remembrance'.

By the middle of the 1980s The Laskett gardens were beginning to impinge on the consciousness of the horticultural world. The gardens themselves still had far to go. But the yew hedges were almost there and that's a landmark. Another turning point was signalled by the decision I took in 1987, after directing two national collections for twenty-two years, to resign the directorship of the V&A and carve out a second career for myself.

In making a new career I was fortunate enough to be a consultant for a few years for the public spaces of Olympia & York, then embarking on its spectacular development of the Canary Wharf site in the Docklands. To that, which ended in 1992, I added through the nineties, and into the early years of the twenty-first century, a piecemeal portfolio of journalism, the writing of popular history, television and, for quite a run, radio. I was, in my fifties, as one reborn: hugely stimulated by having to reinvent myself and keenly aware that having been a director of this or that admirable institution was no guarantee of anything. Less fortunately, Julia gradually ceased to be in demand as a designer. The *verismo* tradition to which she, like Visconti and Zeffirelli, belonged went into eclipse as the deconstruction of the great classics of the repertory became the norm. Her last production was *Beatrix*, a one-hander with Patricia Routledge as Beatrix Potter, at Chichester in 1996.

The bonus side of this was that, for the first time, we truly lived at The Laskett. We could give up that eroding drive back and forth. Julia was most of the time at The Laskett, compiling what surely must be an unrivalled archive on the making of any garden in England since 1945. To every part of the garden she assigned a volume and she mounted up year by year photographs of what it looked like. This runs to some ninety volumes, including some on particular plants or fruit trees. In this she was helped by the advent of cheap photography, which happened during the 1980s. Every picture bears its negative number. We had held on to invoices and kept every sketch I made as the garden was fashioned piecemeal over the decades. In addition my own archives, as well as garden diaries, are considerable. As far as I know there is no equivalent for any other twentieth-century English garden made by people like us, who did not use professional designers but followed our own star. Would that we had such a detailed record for Hidcote or Sissinghurst. If we did we would begin to know what were the sources, ideas and motivation behind their creation. In the case of The Laskett gardens, perhaps uniquely, it is all there.

During this period of relative financial prosperity the garden gained in public reputation. Increasingly I said to Julia: 'We keep on saying that we're going to do this or that but we never do.' This or that was the hard landscaping which up until then we could not afford and which would of course lift the garden yet again on to a higher level. The turning point came when I was sixty and Julia was sixty-five. This was the period of two hugely successful books, *The Story of Britain* (1996) and *The Roy Strong Diaries* (1997), both bestsellers. Now, for the first time, we were able to employ a full-time gardener, in the shape of Robin Stephens. And I was determined that if the garden was to survive (and Julia now had her eye on the National Trust), much needed to be done. Thus began a whole programme of works, many the result of a happy collaboration with Steve Tomlin, who ran an architectural salvage business at Minchinhampton. The Yew Garden was paved and so too was the Elizabeth Tudor Avenue, with the addition of standard hollies and a low inner hedge of yew. Cross paths articulated the Orchard, defining the vistas, and paved the way up to the Kitchen Garden and also to the Rose Garden, where a triumphal arch arose to close the southern vista. Finally, the Rose Garden was paved. New sculptural pieces were also acquired, four of which came from the old Palace of Westminster which burnt down in 1834: a crowned rose; the arms of Edward I; what is likely to be Henry II; and Henry III holding the Shrine of St Edward the Confessor. All of these were purchased in the aftermath of the publication of *The Story of Britain*. This was the period too when Reg Boulton was busy on all the plaques that pointed up the meaning of the various items in the garden, to which we added one on the front of the house *Pax intrantibus* (Peace be to whoever enters this house).

Some of this addition of almost a literary gloss to the garden was inspired by Ian Hamilton Finlay's Little Sparta in the Lowlands of Scotland. This is a garden crammed with meaning, often of quite an abstruse kind. It signalled a revival of the garden of ideas of a kind found in the *fermes ornées* of the eighteenth century. Garden pictures encountered by the visitor are designed to provoke intellectual response in a way utterly alien to the mind of the late twentieth century. The Laskett makes no pretence to that, but does aspire to a more gentle pointing up of meaning and allusion.

Often, allusions have been prompted by a book on which I was working. By now garden history was becoming something of an obsession. The inscription on the pedestal of the Stag in the

Roy and Julia in the Howdah Court, 2003.

Orchard, for example, comes from the description of the Garden of Eden in Milton's *Paradise Lost*:

> . . . a circling row
> Of goodliest Trees loaden with fairest Fruit
> Blossoms and Fruits at once of golden hue
> Appeerd with gay enameld colours mixed.

These verses, which inspired the landscape garden of the eighteenth century, seemed apposite to the Orchard. The Stag looks towards the figure of Britannia, a statue I was prompted to buy in response to the devolution movement and the potential split-up of the island once again into its constituent parts. At the time I was writing *The Arts in Britain* (1999) and came across the earliest reference to Britain in great literature in Virgil's *First Eclogue*, where the poet alludes to this mysterious island as a world of its own set apart from the rest of the known world.

All of this was ongoing and exciting. And then, suddenly, in the summer of 2003, it was discovered that Julia had pancreatic cancer. Within four weeks she was dead. She never saw the paving in the Rose Garden, which she had designed. For her funeral Llanwarne church was, as she had requested, festooned as it would have been for a Harvest Festival. Indeed it occurred on a golden autumn day. The previous day her coffin had been carried through The Laskett gardens and laid, as she had again instructed, in her beloved Orchard, on the vista path to the Stag. Prayers were said by our great friend Canon David Hutt and holy water was sprinkled with a branch of her beloved rosemary. The sense of gathering in and harvest was heightened, as those who came to the funeral were bidden to take home fruits from The Laskett's gardens which ornamented the path to the church. A huge sheaf of Laskett rosemary lay on the coffin. I carried it as we slowly left the church and my last act was to place it back on the coffin at the crematorium.

The garden was not at the top of my agenda in the winter of 2003–4. My immediate focus was again on the house, this time on what needed to be done in order that I could live with comfort in it until I died. From the outset there was never any question but that I would continue to live there. I was sixty-eight and the Strongs tend to live until around ninety, so there was the probability of up to twenty years ahead of me, years which should on no account be wasted. Almost from the moment that Julia died, the impulse in me was to change things. I couldn't live in a shrine. So began the unravelling and reinstatement of the interior of the house.

The garden for this first year went into eclipse. It wasn't until the following October that I could take delivery of her ashes. By then I had commissioned a marble urn in which they would be interred and where I would in time join her. It was sited beneath the Oman quince tree in a quiet corner of her Orchard. It was on 16 October that I at last faced up to placing Julia's ashes, an act of closure. Once again David Hutt presided. I wrote an account of this in my diary:

Was this a winding up or a winding down. It was odd because I was acutely aware that the mortal remains were neither here nor there. That was heightened as I carried those ashes through the garden where her spirit was everywhere. David wore his canonicals and asked me to put together reminiscence and a reading. So I carried them first to one of the Oman quince trees where I read a couple of paragraphs from Julia's article on quinces – beautiful. Next to the new Rose Garden that she had designed where I said a prayer for the departed. Then to the Muff monument and a recollection of our cats and then to the Elizabeth Tudor Avenue and my proposal, a tearful moment of thanks to God for giving her to me. Along and up to the Ashton Arbour where I read the last few paragraphs of *The Laskett* book, on into the Orchard and the urn. My last

reading was the opening of St John's Gospel: 'In the beginning . . .'. David said a few prayers, then lifted the lid and I lowered the container into it. I knelt on the ground and he placed his hands on my head and blessed my new life.

A significant part of that new life was to revolve around the garden. I always encourage those who have lost a partner not to be haunted by guilt if impulses and aspects of themselves that have been muted through the coming together as a couple should resurface. The Laskett gardens were a joint creation with a degree of 'his' and 'hers'. Now everything came under my control. How was I to exercise that control with integrity and also with respect to her memory as the joint maker?

That in a sense was almost decided for me, because during those last months a disease had seized the vast leylandii hedge shutting off the Folly from the rest of the garden. It had to be taken down, a costly exercise, but its removal was a revelation, not only opening vistas to the Hereford landscape but also uniting the garden as a single space. Suddenly light came pouring on to the Elizabeth Tudor Avenue, providing more than a hint as to what I needed to do with the entire garden.

But before that happened the house was reinvented, externally and also internally. Externally, I registered that although the house was early Victorian its proportions were still Georgian, and it would be possible to transform it into a Georgian doll's house. So on to the façade I superimposed pilasters and window embrasures. More importantly, I demolished the 1920s-style bays and replaced them with windows to the ground based on those at a nearby country house, Clytha Park. That signalled a change, a desire to relate house and garden. Julia had been obsessed with privacy, and so every window was heavily curtained and filled with climbing plants. On the odd occasion I showed groups around the garden she retreated and drew every blind in the house firmly down. From the same motive, the front of the house was deliberately obscured by a castellated yew hedge; it could only be approached from the side.

Now all of this was to go in reverse. The castellated hedge was demolished to a set of stumps which, when they sprang again, would be cut into a series of balls. French windows were introduced in the drawing room, letting in light and also giving a delightful vista down to the fountains in the Howdah Court. These decisions about the relationship of house and garden spread out as the Yew Garden paths and the paving in front of the house were widened and a new path which led off the drive presented the façade of the house head on for the first time.

The arrangement of the house internally was also influenced by the desire to place the garden in the forefront. In the drawing room flower paintings and marquetry balanced portraits. In the breakfast room I gathered all my collection of early engravings of formal gardens. The sale of Julia's design library enabled me to commission pictures of the garden, building on the one by Jonathan Myles-Lea which we had commissioned in 1995 and which now took pride of place over the drawing room chimneypiece. Paul Brason, an old friend best known as a distinguished portrait painter, painted an aerial view of the garden as it was, by the time he finished it, in 2009. In relation to that he also produced a large drawing of me as it were dreaming of The Laskett gardens, which stretch out behind me like a vision. Lastly, Richard Shirley Smith produced a mural for the new entrance hall, a capriccio bringing together many of the ornaments and monuments in the garden. So Victoria and Albert, attended by the dog Eos, stroll in from the V&A Temple, Cecil Beaton sits in proximity to his sundial, and Shakespeare presses, pen in hand, away from his monument, while Natalia Petrovna from Julia's ballet *A Month in the Country* glides in behind him. At the centre of the composition there is the Oman All Souls pinnacle as well as some of garden's many inscriptions and, peeping up from below on one side, a beloved cat, Lettice, Lady Laskett. Even if The Laskett gardens were to be swept away tomorrow, they would live on in these pictures.

It was in 2005 that I turned my attention in earnest to the garden itself. I wrote about this in a diary entry in February of the following year which records the activity of the tree surgeons I had brought in.

ABOVE Paul Brason painting his aerial view of The Laskett with, in the background, his drawing of Roy dreaming of The Laskett gardens, 2009.

BELOW Jonathan Myles-Lea's painting, 1996.

Richard Shirley Smith's capriccio, 2006.

The tree surgeons have thinned the cedar and Shaun is replanting the whole area . . . Year two [*sic*] of the arboriculturists . . . Not only the cedar has been sorted out but two massive conifers demolished which flanked the walk to the Oman pinnacle. They then went on to demolish two others in the region of the Flower Garden [at the end of the Serpentine Walk]. The result is a new vista, a new interplay between the various spaces and light, needed so desperately for plants to thrive. On my side the Irish yews along the Elizabeth Tudor Avenue have been reduced to four feet in height thus re-establishing its huge perspective.

So it was that the great cull began, one which was to go on for several years. It was welcomed by the gardeners, who had struggled against overplanting. Over four acres this was a huge enterprise to which basically the winter months were annually given over. Each area in turn called for serious consideration followed by action. The Silver Jubilee Garden, for example, was hemmed in not only by laurels but also by what were now huge conifers. First, all of the conifers were removed and the laurels lowered. This was a garden which in areas quickly went down to rock and therefore most winters was regularly flooded. Eventually I bit the bullet and swept away the existing garden (bar the path which I had laid with my own hands in 1977) and introduced proper drainage, thus paving the way for a box parterre which was to act as a processional way to the Rose Garden. The encircling beds were box-edged and filled with white and yellow roses and lavender.

Not far from there more conifers went, revealing the long-suffering ginkgo tree which I had planted two feet high in 1974 and which had struggled its way up into the light. It remains to be seen whether it will now spread its wings sideways. So much of this felling must be done by eye; often it is only when you have watched a tree vanish that you see what its absence reveals. In this quest the advice and expertise of trained tree surgeons is invaluable. And then there is the decision of when to stop, for too easily all the garden's evergreen verticals can vanish. Without doubt the most radical cull was in the area of the Serpentine Walk. Only two conifers survived out of a small forest, but by then the yew, holly, beech and box topiary had reached maturity. The leylandii behind the Shakespeare Monument were also removed, to be replaced by a laurel exedra matching that behind the Crowned Pillar at the opposite end of the Avenue.

The Colonnade was undoubtedly the greatest structural addition to the gardens, and it came about as a direct result of our opening to the public. The disastrous summer of 2012, when it rained almost without ceasing, made it clear to me that a shelter had to be provided for our visitors. How this could be achieved, on a limited budget, much preoccupied my mind, until it occurred to me that the solution was a classical colonnade, which could form the culmination of the New Walk we had opened up leading from the Fountain Court to the Kitchen Garden. The result shows how much can be achieved with just four reconstituted stone Ionic pillars. Once they were up it was clear that such a grandiose structure could not preside over rows of cabbages and leeks, so the whole area was razed and a formal parterre with Versailles vases surrounded by box hedges was laid out. It then rapidly became apparent that the vast leylandii hedge to the north had to go, opening up vistas to untouched Herefordshire landscape.

I learnt quite early on that a dull hedge can be transformed into an interesting one by cutting it into some shape. It was Rosemary Verey who said to me apropos of the field hedge up the drive: 'You love topiary. Why don't you cut it into something?' So I did. But I never thought that I'd be doing it to hedges I'd planted myself. It is easy to forget that hedges don't only grow from the top. They also grow from below. Together those pressures can radically change a hedge and call for recutting. The two striking examples in the Laskett gardens are the yew hedge in the Rose Garden and the swagged beech hedge linking the limes in the Elizabeth Tudor Avenue. At the entrance to the Rose Garden the hedge had edged its way upwards, obliterating the vista from the steps leading down to the Silver Jubilee Garden. We chopped off a foot. The beech hedge had grown so high that it had reached the level of the first espaliered branches of the limes. Once again the reduction had to be pretty drastic. I knew that yew was virtually indestructible, but the suitability of beech for similar treatment came as a surprise.

It meant that the hedges surrounding the 'rooms' that flank the New Walk to the Colonnade Court could all be reduced by at least two feet and the sides given a similar haircut.

Readers may well wonder why I have not mentioned the dreaded box disease in greater detail. The Laskett was the first to be smitten, with horrendous losses all through the gardens. We are now almost twenty years on from the initial catastrophe and there are few gardens in the country that have not been affected in some way or another by this disease, one which particularly springs to life in a warm damp autumn. Every so often we have another loss, but I am still resolutely planting box. The best advice that I've had so far comes from the head gardener at Holker Hall, and may be summed up in these words: 'You have to live with it.' It is, though, unfortunate that so far the horticultural industry has failed to come through with a start-of-season spray, the kind which is a weak solution of the chemical only officially available to farmers.

In this post-2003 phase little of the garden ornament moved much. Four statues depicting the Arts migrated to give a theme to a garden en route to the Colonnade. Here for the first time a

The house transformed, 2010.

Discussing the garden with Shaun.

concourse area was created and one on a scale open to the sky, air and landscape in such a way as to provide a lung to the contrasting intricacies of the rest of the domain.

There is one final addition I would like to make. Beyond the thuja hedge which acts as a backcloth to the Yew Garden there is a long-abandoned rectangular pond used as a dumping ground. The aim would be to open up that area and move the Lion in the Yew Garden up on to a prominence and make him the source for a trickle of water into a rill running down to the framing central arch of the yew hedge. I see the landscaping as simple and rustic, with perhaps some small flowering trees either side of it emphasizing what inevitably would be another vista.

I used to have a line in any lecture on the garden which ran: 'Remember flowers in a garden are sign of failure.' It always produced, as I hoped, a startled reaction from the audience. Who was this man who dared utter such a horticultural blasphemy? In fact it was designed to make the audience think about the first principles of garden-making, which lie of course in structure and articulation. If all the floriferous areas were put

down to grass or paving The Laskett gardens would still be an intriguing place to explore.

I have never been a plantsman. In contrast, my wife most certainly was. It was she who did the annual order of bulbs, who collected no fewer than ninety-eight varieties of crab apple (which I had, of necessity, to reduce drastically after her death), whose collections of plants such as pulmonarias and bergenias and snowdrops still feature so forcefully in the garden's planting. In the case of her crab apples I bestowed many as gifts to friends to plant in her memory. Others our head gardener, Shaun Cadman, thoughtfully planted at local bus stops in need of a flowering tree. A decade on I often wonder how these are faring and whether they give pleasure to those who travel on the buses.

It was always the formal plantings in which I took the keenest interest, acquisitions such as the six hundred bulbs needed for the parterre in the Silver Jubilee Garden (which, in fact, in recent years have been supplied as a generous gift by my Dutch friend Winfrid de Munck). Then there are the containers in the Yew Garden, tulips in spring and later fuchsias, usually the familiar but excellent 'Tom

Visitors are welcomed and start to explore.

Thumb'. I try to keep a degree of colour control but do not always succeed. The New Borders along the Great Ascent are meant to be muted in tone: they are edged with white cranesbills and planted mostly with monochrome plants such as *Crambe cordifolia* and *Macleaya cordata*. Since opening to the public I find that visitors rejoice at the sight of ordinary old-fashioned garden flowers which they can with ease grow themselves, Michaelmas daisies, *Ligularia, Lysimachia, Anemone* x *hybrida* 'Elegans', *Nepeta, Crocosmia, Helianthus* – an endless but not a very exotic list. I confess to a conversion to grasses. The ground for this was laid by Shaun, who began to sneak them into the borders, and my Damascene moment finally came in a château garden in Belgium where I was dazzled by the sight of *Stipa gigantea* planted against huge undulating yew topiary, a magical reconciliation of new and old. That interest in grasses is reflected above all in the revamped Serpentine Walk, which is an essay in prairie-style planting, swathes of hardy perennials and grasses out of which arise holly, box, yew and beech topiary.

And who, in the new dispensation, maintains the gardens? Shaun, the present head gardener, came in 1997, to be followed, after Julia's death, by Philip Teague. The Laskett gardens are fortunate in having two men who are not only good gardeners but also love the garden as much as I do. They maintain this elaborate four-acre site on just four days a week, so if a weed is visible here and there I make no apology. Rosemary Verey taught me to judge a garden against, among other things, the labour at the disposal of the maker.

Gardens, ephemeral creations, are expensive things to maintain and it was the economic crisis of 2008 which put opening to the wider public firmly on the agenda. It had been open for visits by groups a few times a year, but from 2010 it opened two days a week to prebooked groups of twenty or more (although we found

ways of tucking the odd stray in if we could). From the moment it went public it was a sell-out; for although The Laskett gardens had figured in endless books and articles for over twenty years it had never been fully accessible.

I can truthfully write that even if the garden were razed to the ground tomorrow, nothing can detract from the happiness it has given me and those who work with me. It is an added delight that we have been able to provide pleasure to so many. The last decade has been in a sense the fulfilment of a vision. Initially created as a private Arcadia for owners who wanted a place of escape from the pressures and miseries of public life, the garden has grown into something far richer, a shared joy. That could never have been foreseen in 1973. Nor could it be seen either by so many others who, by chance, have also created remarkable gardens. It is not something that in any sense an amateur gardener can set out to achieve.

There is nothing particularly original in the horticultural repertory of The Laskett gardens, although there may be in their disposition. They reflect a period which shifts away from the heritage decade of the 1970s with its looking back, and moves forward, fuelled by the new discipline of garden history and restoration, into a time of innovation. The gardens are unashamedly nostalgic and romantic and they are emphatically the creation of a marriage of equals. History inspired so much of it – but then it was laid out by a historian and by someone whose designs for the theatre were saturated in a deep knowledge of the past. But it was also created by two people who were keenly conscious of their own history and their own place within contemporary time. I know of no other English garden which resonates so forcefully with the lives of its two makers. This book tells the story of how the surviving creator edited it at the opening of the twenty-first century.

The Remaking

THE CAST

THE AUTHOR

Roy Strong

THE PHOTOGRAPHER

Clive Boursnell

THE GARDENERS

Shaun Cadman

Philip Teague

Maisie

ASSISTANT AND 'GIRL FRIDAY'

Fiona Fyshe

AND OTHER ANIMALS . . .

Lettice, Lady Laskett

Tess

Perkins

Katie

THE BUILDERS

 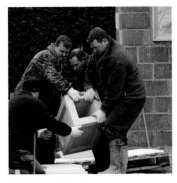 

T&A Building Services – Tom Macklin and colleagues

THE PAINTERS

THE TREE SURGEONS

Paul Reeks and family

Arbor Tree Care & Ross Tree Services – Chris Mawdsley in action

THE ARTISTS

Sculptor, the late Reg Boulton   Sculptor, Catriona Cartwright   Artist, Richard Shirley Smith   Artist, Paul Brason

Shaun and I take regular walks around the
garden to discuss current and ongoing work.

PAX·INTRANTIBVS

VISTAS

The vista north to the V&A Temple through the
Beaton Bridge and the Birthday Garden, in 2006.
The overgrown yew hedge blocked the light and
obscured the Temple.

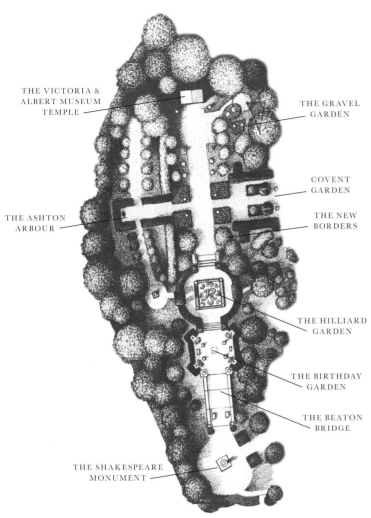

THE VICTORIA &
ALBERT MUSEUM
TEMPLE

THE GRAVEL
GARDEN

COVENT
GARDEN

THE ASHTON
ARBOUR

THE NEW
BORDERS

THE HILLIARD
GARDEN

THE BIRTHDAY
GARDEN

THE BEATON
BRIDGE

THE SHAKESPEARE
MONUMENT

The vista south from the Hilliard Garden to the
Shakespeare Monument, in 2005.

THE SHAKESPEARE MONUMENT, THE BEATON BRIDGE AND THE BIRTHDAY GARDEN

This part of the ascending vista to the Victoria & Albert Museum Temple took several years to come together. The Shakespeare Monument, celebrating the prize I was awarded by the FVS Foundation of Hamburg, came in 1980. Five years later, in 1985, the Birthday Garden was built to celebrate my half-centenary. Julia designed the little garden and gave me the four putti representing the seasons. The linking Beaton Bridge was the fruit of the royalties for my book on Cecil Beaton's royal portraits, published in 1988, and the steps and balustrading went up in 1989.

By 2003 the Portugal laurel and the *Viburnum opulus* planted on either side of the balustrading had shot up to a height of 30 or 40 feet, forming an arcade that framed the Shakespeare Monument to the south. To the north, the yew hedge enclosing the Hilliard Garden cried out to be drastically recut to recapture the view of the V&A Temple.

This was winter work. The *Viburnum opulus* were discarded, but the Portugal laurel were simply reduced to a much lower height. Light now poured in and the planting, which included *Hydrangea quercifolia*, peonies, roses, escallonia and groundcover plants, began to do much better, despite the poor soil. More importantly, the large curved swag taken out of the yew hedge of the Hilliard Garden allowed an enticing view of the Temple from afar. The essentially Italianate nature of this part of the garden was reasserted.

LEFT Renewing the paving around the Shakespeare Monument, which was repainted in shades of stone and terracotta in 2013.

BELOW The vista south from the Birthday Garden to the Shakespeare Monument, before the culling of the *Viburnum opulus*.

RIGHT The putti in the Birthday Garden.

BELOW Katie walks by as Shaun massacres the *Viburnum opulus* and cuts back the Portugal laurel on the Beaton Bridge.

LEFT The Birthday Garden.

BELOW Philip trimming the golden yew.

The Hilliard Garden began its life as a circle of yew planted into the field grass in 1974. Its advance to containing a garden is owed to the royalties from a little book I wrote on the Elizabethan miniaturist Nicholas Hilliard, which was published in 1976. Over the years it went through many changes until, in 1985, when I was fifty, it was paved and a box parterre laid out with our initials J and R. In the late nineties the parterre fell victim to box disease.

However, I was determined somehow to recreate it. This time it was surrounded by a hedge of *Lonicera nitida* 'Baggesen's Gold', a fast-growing plant which looked glorious when the arching sprays of brilliant golden leaves were set against the dark green clipped yew hedging. To the centre composition I added four dwarf conifers as vertical accents and four pedestals with planters containing clipped box.

In the years since 2003 this tiny garden has been subject to little change. Gradually the box matured. The four pedestals and planters migrated to the Silver Jubilee Garden (see pages 110–11) and the yew hedge was divided into two semicircles to afford clear vistas to both the V&A Temple to the north and the Shakespeare Monument to the south. The dwarf conifers will probably be culled in the near future.

The Hilliard Garden, 2013.

THE NEW BORDERS, THE ASHTON ARBOUR
AND COVENT GARDEN

This part of the garden was never much more than a grass walk towards the V&A Temple, punctuated by items from Julia's huge collection of *Malus*. By 2003 the vista was being increasingly impeded. Once the swag in the yew hedge around the Hilliard Garden had been cut, it was clear that the whole approach to the Temple must be more clearly defined.

It was Shaun who suggested that what we needed were flower borders. In addition we decided that the area which was to form the border to the east should have a backing yew hedge to shut out glimpses of the Serpentine planting. The converging lines of perspective were emphasized by globes of golden yew and by a foreground planting of white cranesbills. Otherwise the planting has purposely been kept low-key, so as not to detain or distract the eye. It consists mainly of perennials such as *Macleaya cordata*, phlox, *Crambe cordifolia* and *Anemone elegans*.

The vista from the V&A Temple before the creation of the New Borders.

THE MAKING
OF THE NEW
BORDERS
Discussing the
works; removing
the turf; planting.

The borders are punctuated by the great cross-axis leading from the Ashton Arbour over to Covent Garden and on through the Christmas Orchard into the Rose Garden. The Arbour, planted in 1976 when Julia was working with Frederick Ashton on his ballet *A Month in the Country*, also commemorates their earlier collaboration on *Enigma Variations*. Both had their premieres at the Royal Opera House, Covent Garden. To the Arbour was added, in the late 1990s, a statue from the old Palace of Westminster, of a king whose initial is H, and who is probably Henry II. The entrance to the Arbour is flanked by two urns arising from a froth of bergenia and mophead hydrangeas. None of this called for rethinking, and nor did the 'stage' opposite which we had designated Covent Garden. The yew topiary, beech hedging and standards and the flanking walnut trees frame splendidly a vista through the Orchard to, at its furthest point, the cedar of Lebanon in front of the house.

The vista along the New Borders down to the Shakespeare Monument. The planting has deliberately been kept muted, providing a contrast to the riot of colour along the Serpentine. Globes of golden yew add formal accents.

LEFT The vista from the Christmas Orchard to the Ashton Arbour, 2006.

RIGHT The Ashton Arbour in winter.

FAR RIGHT The vista from the V&A Temple.

BELOW The Ashton Arbour in late summer.

The vista from the Ashton Arbour through Covent Garden to the Christmas Orchard, a tableau of yew topiary globes, peacocks and flanking walnut trees.

THE VICTORIA & ALBERT MUSEUM TEMPLE AND THE GRAVEL GARDEN

The Great Ascent, which was built up in successive sections over the decades, called for a major focal point as its culmination, and that came in the aftermath of my resignation of the directorship of the Victoria & Albert Museum in 1987. The Associates of the Museum, the fundraising association which I had created, presented to me as a farewell gift a witty sculptured plaque by Simon Verity, depicting my profile sandwiched between those of Queen Victoria and Prince Albert (Julia used to say to visitors, 'Victoria is the one without a moustache'). I said when I left the V&A that I would put up a temple to enshrine the plaque and to mark the fourteen years I had spent at the museum. And up it went, with the happy addition of busts of both Queen and Consort.

By 2003 the V&A Temple was demanding reconsideration, as the trellis extensions erected on either side were now nearly twenty years old, and rotten. They were demolished and replaced by a yew hedge in the making. I also created for the Temple a rectangular grass forecourt defined by a low yew hedge. The Temple itself, along with all the other garden ornaments, was painted in shades of stone and terracotta.

The V&A Temple before and after painting, removal
of the flanking trellis and planting of the New Border.

The trellis was removed from either side of the V&A Temple,
and Simon Verity's plaque of Victoria, Albert and Me
was regilded.

The V&A Temple festooned with rose
'Paul's Himalayan Musk'.

The Gravel Garden in 2006 and the beginning of
its transformation in 2008.

The completed Gravel Garden.

To the east of the Temple there was an area designated by Julia as her Nutcracker Garden (she had designed a production of *The Nutcracker* for the Royal Ballet). By 2003 it had become impenetrable. There was no option but to clear the space and start again. But we were not starting from nothing, for the garden had as a background the handsome yew hedge around the Orchard, and there were two splendid trees, one a liquidambar planted just 2 feet high in 1974 and now large, and the other a massive Portugal laurel clipped into a perfect dome (Rosemary Verey said she had never seen a better).

With the determination that whatever was created here should require minimum maintenance, we laid out a gravel garden using different sizes and types of stone. Beneath the trees we planted aconites, which cheerfully push their way up through the stones each spring. Otherwise there is a scattered asymmetrical planting that includes box, holly, cordylines and ferns. A large finial was sited to anchor the composition without distracting the eye from the Temple.

THE ASCENT WEST

THE FOUNTAIN COURT
AND NEW WALK

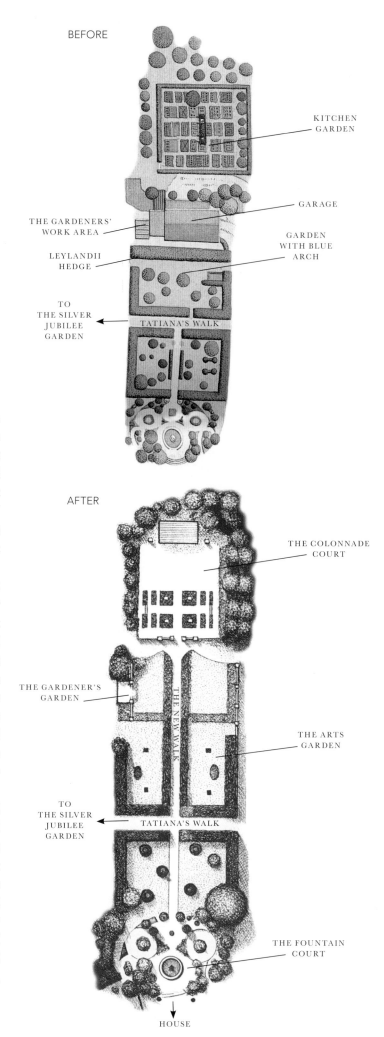

O
ver the years The Laskett had become well known for its spectacular formal vistas, the approach to the Silver Jubilee Garden, the pleached lime avenue we named for Elizabeth Tudor, the vista to the Stag with his gilded antlers, and the long upward ascent to the V&A Temple from the Shakespeare Monument. What was missing was the vista that was potentially the most dramatic of them all, an ascent from the Fountain Court on the west side of the house on and up through the Kitchen Garden. In 2007 I decided that we must finally open up this vista.

At that date the ascent was one long series of obstacles. A short path led from the Fountain Court, but stopped dead where the visitor turned left to descend into the Silver Jubilee Garden. At this point what lay ahead was a long beech hedge, affording access to what lay beyond only through a couple of slight gaps. The area on the other side was never satisfactorily resolved, being a grass rectangle with a blue trellis arch backed by an enormous leylandii hedge planted to obscure the clapped-out 1920s garage behind. Immediately beyond that there was a series of towering conifers and behind them an overgrown field hedge that screened the Kitchen Garden. This project was going to involve a massive clearance operation, certainly the largest I had ever undertaken in the garden.

Countless skips later, we were presented with a blank if battered and muddy space. Early on I had realized that such a large area would need some instant defining features, so where the land rose we built brick curtain walls topped with finials, to emphasize the perspective and act as a screen to the working areas behind. It was important too that the entrance to the Kitchen Garden should be a built structure that would attract the eye from afar. These vertical built elements immediately imposed order on the space, and the flanking walls in addition concealed the slope of the land away from south to north. They also offered attractive backing to beds, one of which faced south and the other,

THE CROWNING OF THE IRISH YEW
A heavy snowfall caused the Irish yews to splinter
and fan outwards. We reduced them to the level of
the surrounding beech hedges. One of the reduced
yews can be seen (below left) as a fountain, covered
against winter frost, is unveiled in spring.

less fortunately, north. In the south-facing bed figs flourished, as did bearded iris 'Sir Roy Strong', which the distinguished jeweller Gerda Flöckinger had bred and named for me.

Every area from the Fountain Court on had to be reconsidered. Around the fountain the four Irish yews were constantly opening up during winter under the weight of the snow, so they were reduced to the height of the beech hedge. The planting around the fountain was also decluttered and two *Malus* 'Julia', named in memory of my wife by Nick Dunn of F. P. Matthews, were moved to be focal points of the two circular flanking beds. The statues representing the Arts were initially re-sited in this area but they were moved yet again (to what became the Arts Garden) when two Roman pillars came from the estate of a friend, the late Joan Griffiths. These pillars provided the perfect frame for the vista up the New Walk. Finally, to the left of the fountain, a new garden was laid out around a topiary yew.

The reordering of the Fountain Court as a frontispiece to the New Walk was perhaps the most significant change. In that recasting the single most important alteration, one fully in accord with the general opening up of the garden, was the removal of the hedge which surrounded the topiary tableau. The beech hedge around that garden had been planted in the middle of the 1970s, but now the topiary pieces had reached maturity the removal of the hedge opened up a splendid panorama that enticed the visitor to explore what lay further up the New Walk. Further on, the hedges were again opened up with a swag, enriching the view either way.

Once the New Walk was excavated it more or less dictated what should happen on either side of it. Beyond Tatiana's Walk, leading down to the Silver Jubilee Garden, there were two spaces which called for definition. They were divided by an ascent. That in fact defined the upper area as a forecourt to the Kitchen Garden. The lower area was reordered into a symmetrical Arts Garden, with the four small statues of the Arts placed to emphasize the sightlines. An inner beech hedge was planted to regularize the area on the southern side. We were surprised to find what a huge difference that made, establishing a balance which had been missing. Then, to separate the hedge from the borders before the entrance to what is now the Colonnade Court, we planted espaliered apples.

Of all the changes we have made, this is the one that has really pulled the garden together, to dramatic effect. It is now possible to walk around almost the whole of the garden, experiencing it as a single unfolding visual.

THE PLACING OF THE
ROMAN PILLARS
The two Roman pillars were a gift
from the estate of Joan Griffiths, a
distinguished picture restorer and
a friend at nearby Peterchurch.
They stand in memory of her and
act as a proscenium arch framing
the Fountain Court and New Walk.

NEW PLANTING NEAR THE FOUNTAIN
To the left of the fountain Shaun laid out a small garden of low-growing plants with a topiary yew as a centrepiece.

ABOVE The fountain
with the front beech
hedge still in place,
but the beech hedge
behind cut through,
giving a glimpse of the
blue arch beyond.

BELOW The fountain
with the return beech
hedge removed,
revealing the topiary
and a bigger view of
the garden with the
blue arch.

The garden with the blue arch and the leylandii hedge concealing the garage.
All of this area was cleared to make way for the New Walk.

Cutting the swag in the beech hedge, 2007.

THE ARTS GARDEN

THE MAKING OF THE ARTS GARDEN
The four statues of the Arts formerly sited in the Fountain
Court were moved into the new themed garden.

The views from the Arts Garden towards the house and to the Colonnade Court (across the espaliered apples).

THE COLONNADE COURT
FORMERLY THE KITCHEN GARDEN

This is the area of the garden that has undergone the most dramatic change in the last few years. The site began in the 1970s as a working kitchen garden, a jumble of beds held in for the most part by railway sleepers with grass paths between, the whole surrounded by a wire fence to keep out the rabbits. To the west and north leylandii hedges were planted to protect the garden from wind and cold; and also, in the case of the western hedge, to hide the A49, which was just a field away. In the centre there was an arrangement of arches supporting a rampant deep pink rose which we always called 'The Gardener's Rose'. This was a part of the garden lovingly tended by my wife and the source of fresh produce for the house.

All that, however, was to change in 2007 when I decided on the New Walk leading from the Fountain Court to this Kitchen Garden. The original intention was that the path should terminate at the entrance but it quickly became apparent that we needed to take it onwards as far as the eye could see. This demanded that the Kitchen Garden should be laid out properly for the first time, a change warmly welcomed by the gardeners. The result was a formal layout redeploying the existing arches at the sides to enhance the perspective. A focal point was provided by a reproduction statue of an eighteenth-century gardener, a piece which acquired a charming individuality when we painted it polychrome. We finally added a picket fence surrounding the entire garden, and painted it blue.

I was tremulous about such radical alterations, as the Kitchen Garden was so closely connected with the labours of my wife. It is true that this part of the garden was always demanding in terms of labour input, and it equally produced vast quantities of vegetables for which I now had no use other than to give them away (a bumper crop of over twenty cauliflowers came close to breaking the camel's back). However, it was for quite another reason that I finally decided it had to go. The appallingly wet summer of 2012 when it seemed to pour with rain non-stop, indicated the urgent need for a substantial building offering cover to our visitors. It was difficult to see how an appropriate solution could be achieved on a limited budget, until I came up with the idea of a classical colonnade. As that rose out of a sea of mud through the sodden winter of 2012 to 2013, it rapidly became apparent that a vegetable garden was hardly an appropriate setting for such a grandiose structure.

The seat is an exact copy of one by Lutyens at Hestercombe, Somerset. It was given to me by Wally Marx. After this picture was taken we added, over the seat, a large inscription by Catriona Cartwright incorporating the initials RS and JTO.

The chaotic but productive old Kitchen Garden.

The new Kitchen Garden under snow,
with Shaun rescuing Katie.

We swept away the cabbages and leeks and laid out in their stead a formal parterre with Versailles vases surrounded by box hedges. That led in turn to the felling of the tall leylandii hedge to the north, opening up spectacular views to the Herefordshire countryside.

The knock-on from all this was considerable. The gardeners' garage and working area was re-sited behind the Colonnade and the area which they had occupied was transformed into the Gardener's Garden – the statue of the gardener being placed on the foundations of the old garage site as a focal point and surrounded by a container plant display. We laid out a new shrub border, a path linking what was now designated the Colonnade Court with the Christmas Orchard and a large circular bed made initially with the idea of its being a small vegetable garden, a notion abandoned when it was seen how inappropriate that would have been. It became a rose garden with a sundial (the most travelled of all the garden's ornaments) as its focal point.

When the whole scheme was finished the alterations seemed almost preordained, giving the garden what it had hitherto lacked, a gracious concourse area. What was more, I am told that the acoustics are good, which opens up the possibility of performance. What began as a piecemeal project has ended as a masterstroke.

The produce that was swept away: raspberries in the fruit cage, squashes and gooseberries. The quince survived as one of several which remain testament to my wife's love of the tree and its fruit.

Laying out the new design for the Kitchen Garden.

New gates and
fencing are
installed and
painted.

THE GARDENER STATUE
The statue is placed and Paul Reeks paints it. It provides an intriguing focal point for the garden.

THE NEW KITCHEN GARDEN
An idiosyncratic mixture of vegetables, flowers, fruit and herbs.

FELLING THE NORTH HEDGE
The hedge to the north, on the right-hand side of
the Kitchen Garden, was removed to reveal the
landscape beyond.

ABOVE The initial scheme for the Colonnade, incorporating the Gardener statue and the two busts of Roman emperors. The drawing is by Gary Grimmit of Haddonstone from sketches I sent him.

BELOW Consideration and discussion with the gardeners and the builder, Tom. As with all garden schemes at The Laskett, adjustments were made as the project progressed.

BOTTOM The site is cleared and the foundations laid for the columns.

Beginning to erect the columns.

Erecting the columns and placing the entablature.
The reliefs are sited and the walls rendered.

Laying the new forecourt paving.

The Versailles vases and busts of emperors
are positioned.

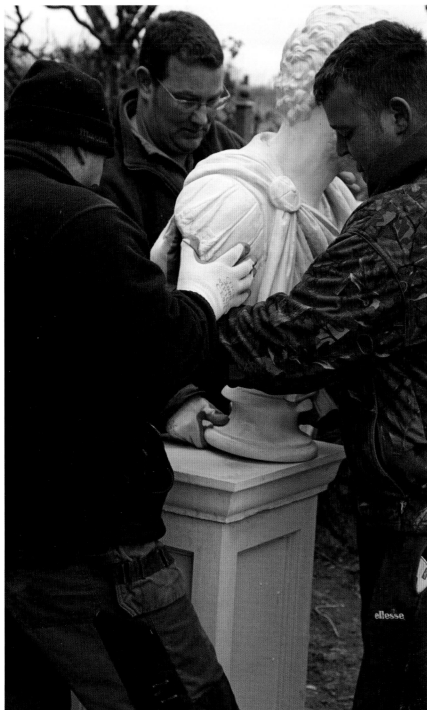

The views north (LEFT) and south (BELOW).
ABOVE First light falls on the Colonnade.

The views east, towards the house, and west, facing the Colonnade.

The transformation of the old gardeners' working area.

The Sundial Rose Garden, incorporating topiary yew from the old Kitchen Garden and a much-moved sundial.

The base on which the garage had stood was paved and given steps and became the Gardener's Garden, the polychrome statue from the old Kitchen Garden acting as a focal point for a growing display of container plants.

THE DESCENT SOUTH

THE SILVER JUBILEE GARDEN

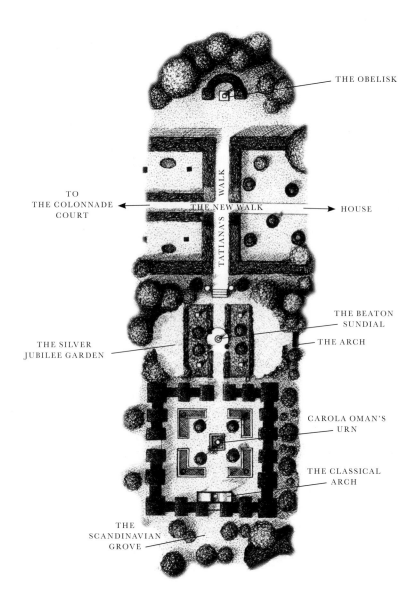

THE OBELISK

TO
THE COLONNADE
COURT

THE NEW WALK

TATIANA'S WALK

HOUSE

THE BEATON
SUNDIAL

THE SILVER
JUBILEE GARDEN

THE ARCH

CAROLA OMAN'S
URN

THE CLASSICAL
ARCH

THE
SCANDINAVIAN
GROVE

In 1974, when I began to plan the Rose Garden, I planted the encircling boundary areas with a variety of conifers including *Chamaecyparis lawsoniana* 'Fletcheri', *Juniperus communis* 'Hibernica' and *Thuja plicata*, along with common laurel. Three years later, in 1977, I laid out the green forecourt beyond the Rose Garden as a garden in honour of the Queen's Silver Jubilee, with a central path of old brick. In 1981 we added an important focal point, a sundial from Sir Cecil Beaton's garden at Reddish House, Broad Chalke. The first planting was entirely white, but it quickly mutated to one of white flecked with violet into purple. The roses at the centre were 'White Pet', while the surrounding borders were filled with 'Iceberg'.

Over the years the thought often occurred that this would have been the ideal site for a parterre – had it not been that the earth on one side went down to rock within a foot, causing an ongoing problem with flooding. But by the year 2000 the garden was becoming increasingly claustrophobic, thanks to the soaring growth of the evergreens. Decisions had to be made. So, piecemeal from 2005 onwards, first we drastically culled the evergreens and then finally we sorted out the flooding problem by introducing drainage. That done, it was possible to reconceive this garden entirely, and lay out the parterre that should have been there in the first place.

The Silver Jubilee Garden in 2005 and 2008.

LEFT The garden on the eve of demolition, 2008.

ABOVE The demolition begins.

TATIANA'S WALK

My wife named this beech-lined path leading to the Silver Jubilee Garden for Tatiana in *Eugene Onegin*. She designed a memorable production of the opera for the Royal Opera House, Covent Garden, in 1971. I went with her to St Petersburg to research the period detail which was always such a feature of her stage work.

The encroaching beech hedge narrowing the path was radically cut back and then lowered in height.

RECOVERING THE
VISTA INTO THE
ROSE GARDEN
The yew hedge,
which had edged
its way upwards
over thirty years, is
radically re-cut.

LAYING OUT THE NEW GARDEN Clearing the old planting, preparing the soil, moving and placing the ornaments and planting the parterre.

THE ARRIVAL OF THE ARCH
The arch was sited to provide a framed vista into
the Silver Jubilee Garden.

The remodelled Silver Jubilee Garden, with its summer planting, in 2013.

THE PIERPONT MORGAN ROSE GARDEN

The Pierpont Morgan Rose Garden was one of the first gardens we created at The Laskett. The money to make it came from my fee for delivering the Walls Lectures at the Pierpont Morgan Library in New York in 1974 – hence its name.

I planted the yew hedge in December of that year to frame a section of what had once been a lawn tennis court. From the outset this has always been a rose garden, though there have been many changes over the decades. The central urn came in 1978, a legacy from Julia's aunt, the writer Carola Oman. Later, I purchased from a garden centre outside Burford the four statues of the Seasons, which we placed in the spandrel beds. In the middle of the nineties, we erected the classical arch with the inscription *Conditor horti felicitatis auctor* ('They who plant a garden plant happiness'), a translation of a Chinese proverb into Latin. Finally, in 2003, the garden was paved with sandstone and the box-edged beds defined with Victorian industrial brick.

For many years the planting was a simple one of old-fashioned roses such as 'Königin von Dänemark' and 'Fantin-Latour', with underplantings of *Alchemilla mollis* and *Astrantia* 'Hadspen Blood'. The urn and the statues were surrounded by purple catmint.

It was opening to the public that triggered replanting. We found we needed a far more extended season of flowering than the old-fashioned roses could give, and in 2011 we came to the decision that we should start again. On the advice of Michael Marriott, David Austin's expert, we opted for the soft pink 'Queen of Sweden', deeper pink 'Maid Marion' and crimson 'Darcey Bussell'. Around the urn we planted the free-flowering creamy pink 'Valentine Heart'. The catmint, never happy in the shady areas of the garden, was replaced with the shade-tolerant *Pulmonaria* 'Sissinghurst White'. *Alchemilla mollis* was retained as part of the underplanting, but with the addition of *Sedum* 'Matrona'. From August right into October this sedum produces soft pink flowers which, if they are left to dry out, continue to look good in winter.

It is often said that you should not plant new roses into soil where roses have previously grown. However, the decision to replant coincided with what amounted to a 'works outing' for the Highgrove garden staff, headed by its very able head gardener, Debs Goodenough. The tip she provided was to plant each new rose in a mixture of good soil and rich compost in a cardboard box sunk into the existing bed. The new roses would be able to develop a vigorous root system which would eventually reach out into the old soil as the box disintegrated. Two years on we see the success of this strategy.

The Rose Garden as it was in 2003.

The old Rose Garden in summer and in winter.

Replanting the garden and trimming the beech.

THE SCANDINAVIAN GROVE

Julia had a love of Scandinavia (she was of Viking descent) and therefore of silver birch trees, and we planted this grove soon after we laid out the Rose Garden. The trees, with their fluttering leaves, never more beautiful than when they turn golden in autumn before their fall, have always been the perfect background to the formal gardens which precede the grove. Here Julia developed a spring garden of hellebores, primulas, fritillaries, crown imperials and pulmonarias which lasted from mid-January to when the trees came into leaf, and then it was over. I moved in an obelisk to add a vertical accent.

OPPOSITE The obelisk in the Scandinavian Grove.

BELOW Moving the obelisk.

THE CHRISTMAS ORCHARD

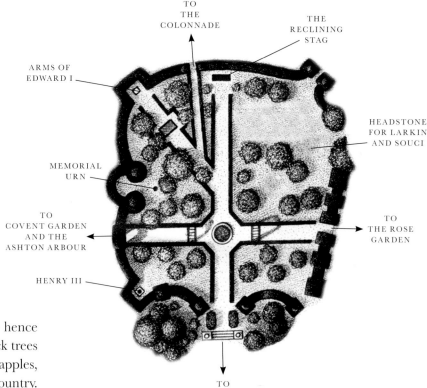

The Orchard was planted just before Christmas 1974 – hence its name. We opted for a collection of dwarfing rootstock trees including plums, gages, damsons and pears but above all apples, as my wife had already discovered that Herefordshire was apple country. Apples became her consuming interest and gradually she assembled a collection of historic varieties. She was later to become equally obsessed by medlars and figs.

However, it was in 1978 that I added a yew hedge enclosing the area, which several decades on now frames it with swags and pilasters defining the two principal vistas, to the Stag with the gilded antlers at the northern end and to Britannia to the south. Beneath the Stag there is a quote from Milton's description of the Garden of Eden in *Paradise Lost*, 'a circling row, Of goodliest Trees . . .'. All of this was given emphasis in the middle of the 1990s when cross paths were laid and low yew and beech hedges defined what was in effect a quartering of the space. Statuary was added: the arms of Edward I and the figure of Henry III holding the shrine of St Edward the Confessor, particularly meaningful to me as I hold the honorary post of High Bailiff and Searcher of the Sanctuary at Westminster Abbey. The Orchard was already well planted with spring flowers, in particular an avenue of *Narcissus* 'Sempre Avanti' leading to the Stag. Standard wisterias and species and other roses were added and, finally, roses were persuaded to clamber up the trees. Shaun has thoughtfully added a garland of snowdrops from my wife's collection around the trees.

Little has been altered in the Orchard. A series of pollarded robinias alongside the Rose Garden hedge have been taken out and a few of the fruit trees, which had reached the end of their life span, have been replaced. But this was always Julia's domain. Within it two slips of the quince tree which grew in the Oxford garden of her grandfather, Sir Charles Oman, took root and flourished. They were to Julia symbolic trees and beneath one of them her ashes rest in a white marble urn bearing her arms and dates. Eventually I will join her.

Here also three of our cats are buried and remembered: William Larkin (named after a Jacobean painter), Sans Souci and, particularly beloved, Lettice, Lady Laskett.

The vista from Covent Garden through the Christmas Orchard
to the Rose Garden, in summer. The pink rose frothing over
the arches is 'Phyllis Bide'. The cross path leads to the Stag.

The Rose
and Crown.

Henry III with the shrine of St Edward the Confessor.

Arms of Edward I.

The Christmas Orchard in spring.

The Christmas
Orchard in
summer.

The Christmas Orchard in autumn.

The Christmas Orchard in winter.

The urn containing Julia's ashes, beneath the quince tree

The Stag.

Britannia.

Avenues and Walks

Shaun cutting the inner yew hedge.

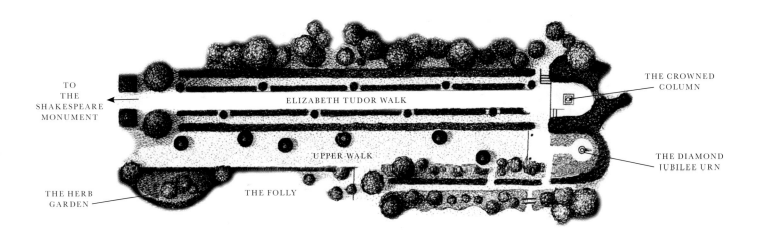

TO
THE
SHAKESPEARE
MONUMENT

ELIZABETH TUDOR WALK

UPPER WALK

THE FOLLY

THE HERB
GARDEN

THE CROWNED
COLUMN

THE DIAMOND
JUBILEE URN

ELIZABETH TUDOR WALK

A great avenue was from the outset part of the overall scheme of the garden. This was to run along what was then the southern boundary. Our first planting was of poplars, but we quickly realized what murderous trees they are, and removed them to the western boundary (where they provide an effective barrier against the winds from the Black Mountains). Next we tried New Zealand beeches. They were killed outright in the great frost of 1981. By this time the pleached lime walk at Sissinghurst had fixed itself in my mind, and I planted the present pleached limes, *Tilia platyphyllos* 'Rubra'. To begin with there were four tiers of branches but – to accommodate my vertigo – they were subsequently reduced to three. For many years the central walkway was of grass with a staggered row of Irish yews and a display of daffodils in springtime. Then in the middle of the nineties we added swagged beech hedges linking the limes, an inner low hedge of Irish yews punctuated with standard hollies (inspired by the one at the National Trust's Westbury-on-Severn) and a checkerboard pathway.

The avenue was intended from the start to have major ornaments as focal points. At the eastern end there is a crowned column, an emblem of Elizabeth I. The column celebrates both Elizabeths, I and II, the pedestal bearing slate plaques with the crowns of the two queens and their initials. However, the crown only arrived in 2002 to commemorate the Golden Jubilee. At the western end a reproduction of an urn designed by William Kent has been customized with plaques by Reg Boulton to mark the FVS Foundation Shakespeare Prize, which was awarded to me in 1980.

By 2003, however, it was clear that the avenue was calling for radical treatment. To the south a mammoth leylandii hedge shut out the Folly. Looking north nothing could be seen through the pleached limes except more conifers and evergreens. At the western end, the Shakespeare Monument was backed by another forest of quick-growing conifers. Even the relatively new additions called for attention. The Irish yews had soared to the top of the pleached limes, destroying the perspective, and the swagged beech hedges had edged their way up so that in summer they joined the leaves of the limes, forming an impenetrable wall.

The first to yield to the axe were the leylandii, both at the southern end and to the west. The former opened up a whole new area of the garden to be developed (see page 152) and also let light flood on to the walkway. Eventually this would afford views through to a new topiary garden and a major mixed border (see page 155). This was followed by a similar cull to the north, conifers and other evergreens falling to open up glimpses of the garden up to the Orchard. All of that was helped enormously by a savage recutting of the swagged beech hedge. In addition the Irish yews were radically reduced in height, thus restoring the dramatic perspective of the avenue.

Elizabeth Tudor
Walk in winter.

RIGHT Shaun beheading the Irish yew
– and me, having beheaded the first to
show the gardeners that was really what I
wanted them to do!

FAR RIGHT Elizabeth Tudor Walk in
springtime, with the perspective restored
by the reduction of the yew, but before
a similar execution of half the standard
hollies had emphasized it further.

RESTORING THE BEECH HEDGE
The swagged beech hedge and the pleached limes
form a gold wall of foliage. Shaun measures the
swag and begins the cutting.

Clearing and tidying up.
Order is restored with the vistas through to the
pleached avenue and beyond re-established.

BELOW LEFT Paul repaints the column (once ochre and blue) in stone and terracotta.

BELOW RIGHT The column repainted. Shaun trims the laurel hedge, 2013.

The avenue in 2013. Philip trims a holly.

THE UPPER WALK

It was indeed the leylandii hedge to the south of the Elizabeth Tudor Avenue that acted as the accidental catalyst for much of the culling in the garden. This hedge, which we had planted when we first came to The Laskett, was after thirty years of growth 65 yards long and 15 feet high. In 2003 it was hit by disease and had to be taken out. With its passing, light poured into the garden, making me realize that the mass planting of conifers had in the long run rendered much of The Laskett gloomy and claustrophobic.

In the space left by the hedge, I was able to develop a large mixed border of shrubs and perennials whose serpentine shape echoed that of the swagged beech opposite and also the curves of the low hedge behind of field maple, golden privet and beech. The large area between was grassed and into it I moved topiary specimens which I was in the process of training. The shock of removal halted their growth, but once settled they quickly came to maturity. Overall this resulted in an asymmetrical vista in contrast with the precise geometry of the Elizabeth Tudor Walk. A sundial was placed as a focal point, but it was never satisfactory here. This ornament was eventually to find its resting place at the centre of the new rose bed in proximity to the Colonnade (see page 97).

The Upper Walk in 2007, after the demolition of the leylandii hedge.

The Upper Walk in winter, with Shaun and Philip pleaching the limes.

Culling trees.

The new border and topiary in the making.

Emboldened by the removal of the leylandii hedge, I decided to take out one of the large trees on the perimeter of what we were now calling the Upper Walk. Once again light flooded in.

There was, however, something always unresolved about this area until, in 2012, I was presented with a cast of a famous garden ornament, Pope's Urn. I was determined to transform this into the centrepiece of a tableau which would celebrate the Diamond Jubilee of the Queen. Painted in Pop Art blue and yellow, with an appropriate inscription cut by Catriona Cartwright on a slate plaque, the urn was sited in a circle of sandstone with a short approach path flanked by Irish yew and two finials. The whole is set against a hedge of clipped laurel and in summer four containers with standard bay trees are added. The composition comes together to form a tableau complementary to the crowned column nearby.

Installing the
Diamond Jubilee
Urn, 2012.

The vista to the Diamond Jubilee Urn, 2013.

THE HERB GARDEN

This area on the edge of the garden next to the Folly was overplanted with trees almost to the point of suffocation. Another radical clearance was needed. As it faced south we decided to make a herb garden here, with a scattering of ornaments to hold it together. This was the first place we used terracotta, a colour that was subsequently to spread all through the garden. Six years on, this area has not proved entirely successful as a home for herbs, so it is likely to change function once more.

BELOW Laying out the Herb Garden.

RIGHT The Herb Garden in 2007.

THE SERPENTINE

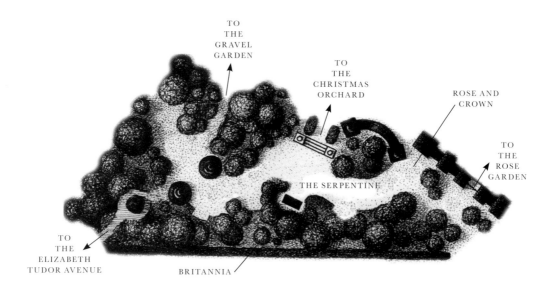

From the mid-seventies, when the earliest plans were drawn up, we intended this area to be articulated by a winding grass walk which would offset the preponderance of straight avenues and vistas in the design as a whole. Its inspiration was to be found in engravings of late seventeenth-century wildernesses, enclosures filled with winding paths used for exercise. The walk began its life with flower borders on either side but these borders were quickly abandoned as too onerous to maintain. It then became a grass path edged with daffodils in spring and backed on both sides by conifers and largely evergreen shrubs. By the late 1980s flowers had returned to one end of it, together with pergola arches bearing roses. That was in response to writing garden design books, for which I needed to learn something about flowers. ('And about time too,' Rosemary Verey remarked.) Topiary in yew, holly and box also punctuated the route, as well as some of Julia's fruit trees. Later came the statue of Britannia to complete the vista from the Orchard. To Britannia was added a line from the Roman poet Virgil's *First Eclogue*, 'Et penitus toto divisos orbe Britannos', the first reference to Britain in great literature, a line which cast the island and its inhabitants as a mysterious world apart – 'cut off as they are by the whole width of the world'. Always called the Serpentine, this path had, with its twists and turns, the ability to surprise.

This came very near top of the list of areas in need of remaking, for in places it had become overwhelmingly claustrophobic. Starting in about 2005, we razed almost the whole of the original planting, retaining only the topiary, a few lower-limbed conifers for height, and a few specimen trees, like the *Acer griseum* and the mulberry. Light flooded in. The grass walk was replaced by a path of sandstone stepping stones. Further minor gravel paths led northwards up to the Gravel Garden or south to Elizabeth Tudor Avenue. The pleached limes in Elizabeth Tudor, now visible, would act as a geometric background to what was to become a large prairie-style planting. Within two or three years the garden which for decades had been so flower-shy suddenly became floriferous, with a wavy sea of grasses interspersed with drifts of acanthus, lysimachia, ligularia, crocosmias, heleniums, helianthus, nepeta, Michaelmas daisies, and much more.

Britannia,
before and after
the clearing of
the area.

Clearing trees from the Serpentine.

The making of the new path.

Planting the New Border.

Making a formal ascent to the south.

Clearing and planting the area to the north.

THE NEW PLANTING

A winding path of sandstone is flanked by massed plantings of easily grown perennials including eupatorium, Michaelmas daisies, hardy geraniums, nepeta, acanthus, cleome, heleniums, helianthus and crocosmias, all intermingled with grasses – miscanthus, pennisetum and stipa varieties. Above them rise box, yew, privet and holly topiary.

The new planting offers the pleasure of looking from profusion over towards the formal vistas where geometry prevails. Architectural accents such as the piers and the statue of Britannia act as anchors amidst the turbulence of the plant explosion.

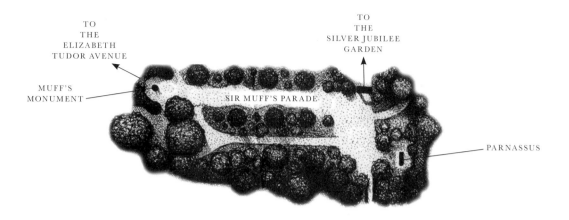

MUFF'S
MONUMENT

SIR MUFF'S PARADE

TO
THE
SILVER JUBILEE
GARDEN

PARNASSUS

Gardens on this scale when they are conceived somewhat piecemeal tend to end up with odd areas here and there demanding resolution. Disregarded for years, this space between the Pierpont Morgan Rose Garden and the drive was where a succession of builders was bidden to dump any earth excavated from elsewhere. For years, apart from the rubbish heap, there was nothing here other than a green walk with a row of crab apples on one side and pollarded robinias on the other, culminating in a large clipped yew which had come as a gift from Sutton Place, a reminder of my role as a trustee there. Eventually a bust of Diana on a plinth became a focal point. On the other side of the yew there was an 'antechamber', a small enclosure in which one of our great cats was buried, the Revd Wenceslas Muff. He rests here in proximity to this walk which he used to patrol, hence its somewhat eccentric designation.

Eventually, at the close of the 1990s, this area finally got some attention. A path was laid from the drive. The rubbish mound was given steps, and arches festooned with roses. The views it afforded across the garden and out to the landscape were a bonus. The space between here and the hedge up the drive was infilled with trees, including silver birch, and underplanted with snowdrops and cowslips. Flower beds with a mixed planting were added on either side of the grass walk, and the bank at the end nearest the house was landscaped and given a trellis arbour with a seat. Renaissance gardens always had a mound of some kind, usually called Parnassus to signal that the house and garden were a home for the Muses and hence the cultivation of the Arts. Therefore the name.

But this was another area which was overcrowded with conifers, and crying out for light and air. And so, in 2010, down they all went. The light poured in and suddenly a luckless ginkgo which we had planted in 1974 was revealed, a slender specimen that had been struggling its way upwards ever since. In the reordering of the Silver Jubilee Garden Diana migrated there. Parnassus lost its seat and exploration through the dense growth of shrubbery behind it revealed that the arch which framed the seat would, once all of this was cleared, open up a handsome vista to the Fountain Court.

Sir Muff's Parade.

Reg Boulton's tomb for the
Revd Wenceslas Muff.

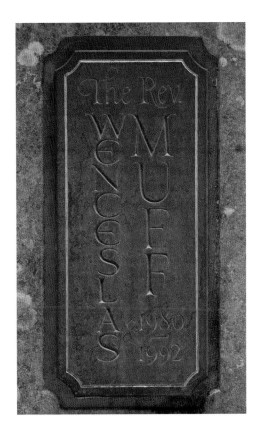

LEFT Moving Diana.

RIGHT The vista along the raised bank leading south towards Muff's Monument and the entrance to Elizabeth Tudor Walk. From here there are views down to flower borders and to a naturalized area where silver birches tower above a springtime carpet of snowdrops and cowslips.

Parnassus: clearing the vista to the Fountain Court.

The vista revealed.

The Gardens about the House

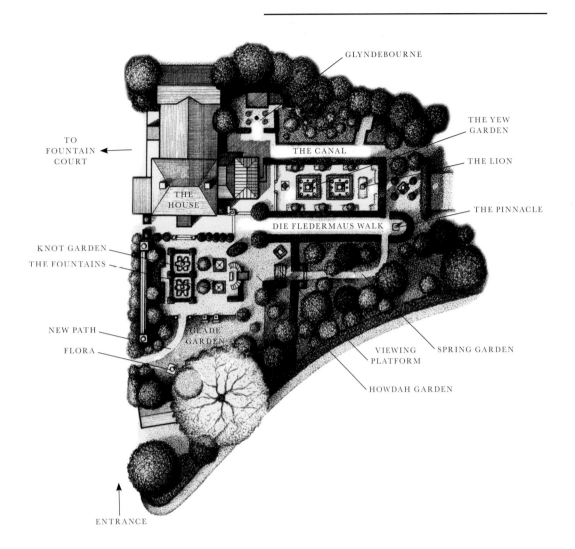

GLYNDEBOURNE

THE YEW GARDEN

TO FOUNTAIN COURT

THE CANAL

THE LION

THE HOUSE

THE PINNACLE

DIE FLEDERMAUS WALK

KNOT GARDEN

THE FOUNTAINS

NEW PATH

GLADE GARDEN

FLORA

VIEWING PLATFORM

SPRING GARDEN

HOWDAH GARDEN

ENTRANCE

BELOW LEFT Shaun pruning the drive border.

BELOW RIGHT Fiona clears the steps in front of the shop before visitors arrive.

RIGHT Vista across a gate pier towards the house.

BELOW The main drive to the house with shaped beech trees, yew and box topiary.

THE YEW GARDEN

The Yew Garden was one of our earliest plantings, in 1974. By the middle of the 1990s it had developed into a large box parterre which was destroyed at the close of that decade when *Cylindrocladium buxicola* rampaged through the garden. All the infected plants had to be ripped out and burnt. To replace what we had lost my wife designed a simple parterre of green and golden yew, the latter a generous gift from a gardening friend. Standards of golden yew were planted at the centre of this garden to echo the clipped *Amelanchier lamarckii* at its edge and the hawthorn flanking the statue of the lion from the Houses of Parliament which terminates the vista from the house.

Of all the garden areas at The Laskett the Yew Garden is perhaps the one that has undergone least change over the past decade. The paths have been widened, two of the amelanchiers have been removed to enhance the perspective and a planting of *Anenanthele lessoniana* (syn. *Stipa arundinacea*) has been added to the existing *Stachys byzantina* in the perimeter beds. The parterre is enlivened and given colour with spring and summer container plantings of tulips and fuchsias.

DIE FLEDERMAUS WALK

Named for a production my wife designed of Strauss's operetta for the Royal Opera House in the 1970s, Die Fledermaus Walk leads the eye to a pinnacle from Nicholas Hawksmoor's eighteenth-century restoration of All Souls College, Oxford. This pinnacle was a gift to Julia's grandfather, the historian Sir Charles Oman, who was a Fellow of All Souls. It was for some years positioned outside his house in Oxford, before migrating first to the Putney house of his son, Julia's father, Charles Chichele Oman, Keeper of Metalwork at the Victoria & Albert Museum; and then, finally, to The Laskett. It was precious to my wife as a memorial of her distinguished family and so I set it on a pedestal and commissioned Reg Boulton to sculpt the plaque which carries the Oman arms and the initials of both father and son. The walk, a long gallery of yew and beech, had two conifers as its sentinels but by 2003 they had far outgrown their welcome. Down they came. Later the beech hedge was recut to match the curves in the yew.

THE SPRING GARDEN

An odd unresolved triangle of garden directly south of the Yew Garden, in which early on I planted some *Cupressus arizonica*, pretty grey-blue conifers now soaring high. It never developed into anything much more than a walk-through, but we called it the Spring Garden because of the grass dappled with spring flowers. In an attempt to achieve some structure I added a winding gravel path, more topiary and, beneath the junipers, beds planted with tulips and rosemary. Lowering the boundary hedge in an effort to open up a view of the landscape proved a failure, as the farmer's hedge opposite still blocked the outlook. The most significant change was the recutting of the beech hedge to the west, a reduction of some 5 feet that provided a vista to the remodelled façade of the house.

LEFT The conifers were removed from Die Fledermaus Walk and the beech hedge was lowered.

RIGHT The Spring Garden.

THE HOWDAH GARDEN

Our earliest planting in the area in front of the house, in 1974, consisted of a small procession of *Juniperus communis* 'Hibernica'. The junipers eventually flanked a knot garden which was laid out in the early nineties, initially of box enclosed by low yew hedges and infilled with coloured glass and gravels, but latterly, after the knot was destroyed by *Cylindrocladium buxicola*, of golden and green heather. The statue of Flora arrived in 1990.

The whole of this area changed dramatically in the late nineties with the addition of the so-called Howdah, a viewing platform designed by my wife and composed of architectural salvage, including Victorian radiator panels and spiral staircases. The summit offers stunning views across the Herefordshire landscape towards Gloucester. At its feet nestle two fountains and a number of bears sculpted by a friend, Astrid Zydower, for a display in the Orangery at Warwick Castle. When the display was taken down we rescued a number of them and deployed them in the garden.

The façade of the house was partly concealed by a crenellated yew hedge which I planted more or less on arrival. As a consequence there was no dialogue between the garden and the interior of the house, nor any means whereby the visitor might view its façade head-on. Although the house was built about 1835 it preserved Georgian proportions, which I longed to strip of superfluous excrescences. I began by demolishing the rotten old porch and the flanking 1920s bay windows, replacing them with a new porch and two windows to the ground copied from ones at nearby Clytha

OPPOSITE The knot garden and the façade of the house before the changes.

BELOW The Howdah Garden after the main changes but before the colour was altered to terracotta and stone.

Park. Embrasures were added to the upper windows and two massive pilasters framed the entire façade. Between the windows there were slate ovals on which Reg Boulton had sculpted our coats of arms.

Rosemary Verey had commented on her last visit to The Laskett that the junipers were reaching the end of their lifespan, so I took them out, allowing a clear view of the remodelled façade. The crenellated yew hedge was demolished to a series of stumps, which, when they sprang again, we cut into low spheres. We widened the paths on either side of the knot and made a new curved path from the drive. This meant that the house could now be viewed from afar. We also lowered the encircling hedge, opening up another view out into the landscape.

It had for years been apparent that it was impossible to grow anything beneath the great cedar, so we gravelled the area and laid steps leading to a seat affording a panorama of the house and front garden. Everything again changed dramatically when most of the garden structures and ornaments were painted terracotta and stone instead of blue and ochre. Finally, in 2012, we painted the house cream and Oxford blue.

A winter
panorama before
the changes.

The crenellated yew hedge was reduced to stumps which, when they sprang back again, were cut into spheres.

Resculpting old hedges.

OVERLEAF
Flora and the panorama looking towards
Gloucester, before the lowering of the hedge and
the removal of the holly finials.

OPPOSITE The Howdah, like most of the other garden structures, became stone and terracotta instead of blue and ochre.

BELOW A view from the platform looking past the house towards the New Walk and the Arts Garden.

The house today.

BIBLIOGRAPHY

ARTICLES

Rosemary Verey, 'Growing Strong', *Homes and Gardens*, November 1987, pp. 102–7 (reprinted in *Australian Vogue Living*, October 1988)

Graham Rose, 'A Lesson in Making Space', *Sunday Times*, 23 July 1989

'Dramatic Art', *The Gardener*, February 1990, pp. 28–31

'Growing Strong', *Woman's Journal*, August 1991, pp. 126–31

Richard Rosenfeld, 'Strong Lines', *Country Homes and Interiors*, Christmas/New Year, 1992, pp. 84–7

Stephen Lacey, 'Sweetness from the Strongs', *Daily Telegraph*, 11 January 1992

Lucia Green, 'With this garden I thee cherish . . .', *Sunday Express Magazine*, 27 September 1992

Chris James, 'A Strong Sense of History', *Practical Gardening*, pp. 46–9

Andrew Lawson, 'Strong Imagination', *House & Garden*, March 1993, pp. 88–91

Roy Strong, 'The Laskett: The Story of a Garden', *Hortus*, 1992

Jonathan Dawson, 'A Room with a Yew', *Sunday Express*, 30 October 1993

David Wheeler, 'Pomp and Circumstance', *Country Living*, October 1994, pp. 100–103

'Mein Garten – mein Königreich', *Garten*, Spring 1997

Patrick Bowe, 'Fantasy from a Common Field', Centenary Issue of *Country Life*, 16 January 1997, pp. 56–63

Elspeth Thompson, 'Roy's Own Story', *Sunday Telegraph Magazine*, 4 May 1997, pp. 32–5

'Herefordshire Garten der Erinnerung', *Schoner Wohnen Decoration*, 3, 2000, pp. 124–9

Jacky Hobbs, 'Great Gardeners: Sir Roy Strong', *Gardens Monthly*, December 2003, pp. 37–40

Vanessa Berridge, 'A Garden of Passions', *The English Garden*, March 2004, pp. 6–13

Chris Young, 'The Age of Elegance', *Garden Design Journal*, July/August 2004, pp. 36–9

Chris Young, 'Coming of Age', *The Garden*, June 2006, pp. 414–19

Roy Strong, 'After She'd Gone', *Guardian Weekend*, 21 October 2006, pp. 116–17

Stephen Anderton, 'The Tastemakers', *The Times*, 17 May 2008

Stephen Anderton, 'The Light Programme', *Sunday Times*, 22 June 2008, pp. 42–3

Anne Wareham, 'The Emperor's New Clothes', *The Spectator*, 29 October 2011

BOOKS

Rosemary Verey, *The Garden in Winter*, Frances Lincoln, 1987, pp. 9, 16–17

'The Garden as Personal Biography, full of Wit and Drama', in Caroline Seebohm and Christopher Simon Sykes, *Private Landscapes*, Clarkson N. Potter Inc., 1989, pp. 158–9

Anne Scott-James, *Gardening Letters to my Daughter*, Michael Joseph, 1990, pp. 89–91

Roy Strong, *The Roy Strong Diaries 1967–87*, Weidenfeld & Nicolson, 1997, passim

'A Garden Autobiography', in Anita Pereire, *Gardens for the 21st Century*, Aurum Press, 1999, pp. 72–6

Ursula Buchan, *The English Garden*, Frances Lincoln, 2000, pp. 42–3, 245–56

Tessa Traeger and Patrick Kinmouth, *A Gardener's Labyrinth: Portraits of People, Plants & Places*, Booth Clibborn Editions, 2002, pp. 84–91

Roy Strong, *The Laskett: The Story of a Garden*, Bantam Press, 2003 (paperback 2005)

The Oxford Companion to the Garden, ed. Patrick Taylor, Oxford University Press, 2006, s.v. The Laskett

Timothy Mowl and Jane Bradney, *Historic Gardens of Herefordshire*, Redcliffe, 2012, pp. 265–8

'The Laskett', in Tim Richardson, *The New English Garden*, Frances Lincoln, 2013, pp. 296–309

A new arrival
waiting to be sited.